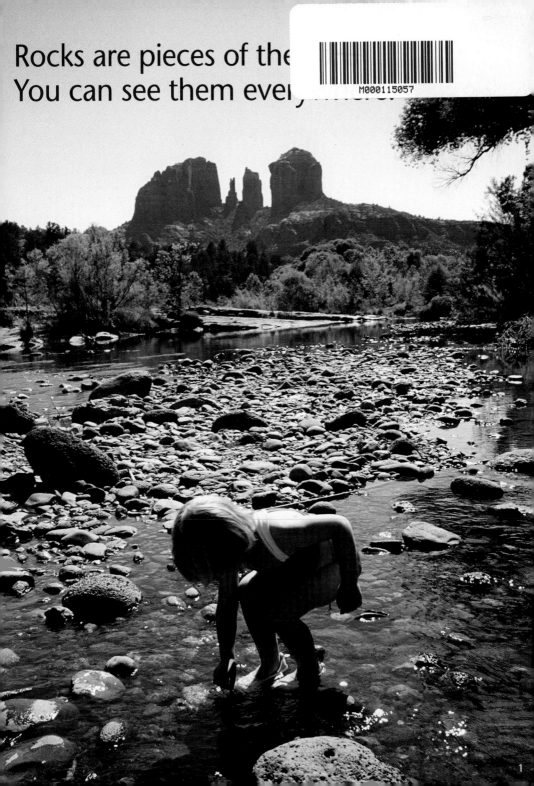

Rocks are pieces of the
You can see them every

You can find a big boulder
on a rocky hill.

You can find small rocks
and pebbles near rivers
and streams.

On the beach,
you can find
tiny grains of
sand. These
are rocks, too.

In the desert, you can find tall rocks that reach up to the sky.

You can collect rocks to study their different colors, patterns, and shapes.

Most rocks are very old. Some even show traces of plants and animals that lived long ago. These traces are called **fossils**.

Rocks are strong and useful.
The ancient Egyptians used many
rocks to build these huge pyramids.

People used rocks to make all these things, too!

11

Do you see anything made
from rocks in this picture?

Soil is made from tiny pieces of rock mixed with **humus**.

Humus is formed when leaves and other living things decay and begin to break apart.

Plants, animals, and people
all depend on soil to live.
Plants grow in soil.

Animals eat
plants.

People also eat food grown from plants.

Did you know that rocks and soil gave us so many gifts?